Rebuke &
Challenge

Rebuke &
Challenge

The Point of Jesus' Parables

Norman H. Young

REVIEW AND HERALD PUBLISHING ASSOCIATION
Washington, DC 20039-0555
Hagerstown, MD 21740

This book was
Edited by Richard W. Coffen
Designed by Richard Steadham
Type set: 11/12 Bookman

PRINTED IN U.S.A.

Library of Congress Cataloging in Publication Data

Young, Norman H., 1938-
  Rebuke and challenge.

  1. Jesus Christ—Parables. I. Title.
BT375.2.Y68   1985   226'.806   85-14521

ISBN 0-8280-0286-X

Affectionately dedicated to

my wife, Elisabeth,

and

our children, Paul and Michelle

Contents

Foreword

Jesus' parables are great works of art, created by a Master-craftsman. It is, therefore, presumptuous to attempt to clarify them. Such an undertaking implies that the expositor sees himself as more skilled than the Originator. Accordingly, some defense of this book is necessary. Two reasons, I believe, justify the following pages. First, works of art are designed to stimulate thought and discussion, and Jesus' parables are no exception. This book contains the results of such stimulus as I have received from my own study of the parables, and the Review and Herald Publishing Association publishes it as part of an ongoing discussion. Second, Jesus told His parables long ago in a culture quite different from ours. Some elucidation of the historical circumstances of the parables is therefore vital. This volume explains to modern-day readers some of the cultural background to the parables.

This is a semipopular book. Consequently I have tried to avoid the detailed analysis of the various possibilities that the text sometimes presents. Scholars delight in such minutiae to the point of mania, but ordinary readers get bored with them. As a result, I have not referred to debated items such as the following: whether or not Simon in the parable of the two debtors insulted Jesus; whether "tax collector" in the parable of the Pharisee and the publican refers to a Jewish hireling of the Romans or a Hellenistic entrepreneur, or whether "with himself" in the same parable goes with "stood" or "prayed"; and whether one should translate Luke 18:5 as "finally wear me out" (T.E.V.) or as "her continual coming."

At this stage in parable research, convincing originality is difficult. You will find very little that is new in the following pages. I owe a large debt to the works of T. W. Manson, J. Jeremias, K. E. Bailey, and E. Linnemann. I have not ignored the newer approaches of, for example, R. W. Funk, J. D. Crossan, and D. O. Via, Jr., but I have seldom followed them.

Thanks are due to D. Hokin for typing my unreadable handwriting, and to R. Coffen and D. Hansen for editing and improving my style.

Introduction

Christians often misunderstand Jesus' parables in one of two ways. One is an ancient error, and the other is modern.

First, from the days of the Church Fathers, many Bible readers have interpreted Jesus' parables as allegories. Allegory imposes upon Jesus' stories the doctrines of the church. Allegory finds theological significance even in isolated words or incidents. For example, Augustine identified the wounded man in the parable of the good Samaritan as Adam. The man's misfortune on the Jericho road, he related to the Fall. The inn represented the church. The innkeeper was the apostle Paul, the pack animal stood for the incarnate flesh of Christ, and so on. Expositors in the Middle Ages actually saw the sacraments (the Catholic Church's remedies for sin) in the oil and the wine with which the Samaritan treated the robbed man's wounds.

Second, since the nineteenth century the parables of Jesus have too often been sentimentalized into moral stories suitable for children. Until recently, modern expositors regarded the parables as simple tales that Jesus told in order to present a single, general moral maxim. They thought of

11

Jesus as an innocuous popularizer of homely truths. Unlike allegory, which proposes multiple meanings, this approach insists that each parable makes only one general point.

Such an understanding of Jesus' parables agreed with the common nineteenth-century belief that our Lord was a teacher of simple ethical truths. Scholars in this period often charged Paul with changing Jesus' straightforward teaching into a difficult and obscure theology of redemption. The Irish playwright George Bernard Shaw, for example, described Paul's role as a "monstrous imposition . . . upon the soul of Jesus" ("Preface on the Prospects of Christianity," in *Androcles and the Lion*, p. 79). H. G. Wells, the English science-fiction writer, put it equally bluntly: "What Jesus preached was a new birth of the human soul; what Paul preached was the ancient religion of priest and altar and the propitiatory bloodshed."— Quoted in M. Muggeridge and A. Vidler, *Paul: Envoy Extraordinary*, p. 14. Nietzsche, the German philosopher, was convinced that Paul had replaced the simplicity of Christ's example, teaching, and death with theological ideas of atonement and resurrection (*The Antichrist: An Attempted Criticism of Christianity*, para. 41, 42).

All such ideas reflect the teaching of F. C. Baur, the German theologian who founded what is now usually called the Tübingen School. As a Biblical scholar, Baur defended the idea that Paul moved away from the simple ethical principles of Jesus toward the dogmas of organized Christianity (that is, the Trinity, Incarnation, et cetera). This book opposes such views. Jesus' parables are not so straightforward and untheological as many have popularly thought. Also, in passing, I contend that Paul faithfully preserved Jesus' teaching as found in the Gospels.

Both the treatment of the parables as allegories and the interpretation of them as stories with a single moral point have the same fault. Each approach ignores the historical circumstances in which Jesus first told His parables. We should read the parables within the context of Jesus' cut-and-thrust debates with the religionists of His day. In fact, Jesus' parables stirred up such anger in some quarters that His opponents ultimately had Him crucified. That is not the end one would expect were Jesus merely a spinner of moral tales.

Christ did not relate His parables in order to materialize some abstract philosophical truth or to immortalize some religious platitude. Nor did He wish to entertain His listeners. With His parables Jesus (1) challenged religious smugness, (2) proclaimed God's salvation to the rejected, (3) invited the despised to God's banquet, and (4) reversed the opinions of pious bigotry. Jesus' parables belong, in the main, to the heat of real controversy. One can detect in them the pungent smell of "gunpowder."

The parables are, therefore, neither allegories that picturesquely codify the systematic doctrines of the church nor preambles that lead to a general moral conclusion. Each is an organic whole and each originated in dialogue with a living audience. Those who heard one of Jesus' stories could not remain mere listeners. They were compelled to become involved within the parable and on its own terms. The inner power of the story generally forced the hearers to assume one of the roles within it. Inevitably this experience challenged and scrutinized their own prejudices and religious presuppositions. The parable's punch line always left the audience with an uncomfortable demand for decision and change.

To describe the parables as simple narratives is hardly accurate. Despite their natural charm, Jesus' parables deal with powerful and controversial issues—not abstractly, but in the heated language of religious conflict and dispute. Even today few readers can readily remain detached from the serious challenge of the parables. The superficial reader will, of course, discern only the story. Others who penetrate deeper will either be angered or overjoyed by Jesus' message. Since the parables often question the very grounds for the spiritual confidence of religious man, it is he rather than the obvious sinner who usually enters the conflict. The challenge of the parables, however, confronts sinner and saint alike.

CHAPTER 1

The Two Debtors

Luke 7:36-50

36 One of the Pharisees asked him to eat with him, and he went into the Pharisee's house, and took his place at table. ³⁷And behold, a woman of the city, who was a sinner, when she learned that he was at table in the Pharisee's house, brought an alabaster flask of ointment, ³⁸and standing behind him at his feet, weeping, she began to wet his feet with her tears, and wiped them with the hair of her head, and kissed his feet, and anointed them with the ointment. ³⁹Now when the Pharisee who had invited him saw it, he said to himself, "If this man were a prophet, he would have known who and what sort of woman this is who is touching him, for she is a sinner." ⁴⁰And Jesus answering said to him, "Simon, I have something to say to you." And he answered, "What is it, Teacher?" ⁴¹"A certain creditor had two debtors; one owed five hundred denarii, and the other fifty. ⁴²When they could not pay, he forgave them both. Now which of them will love him more?" ⁴³Simon answered, "The one, I suppose, to whom he forgave more." And he said to him, "You have judged rightly." [44]*Then turning toward the woman he said to Simon, "Do you see this woman? I entered your house, you gave me no water for my feet, but she has wet my feet with her tears and wiped them with her hair.* [45]*You gave me no kiss, but from the time I came in she has not ceased to kiss my feet.* [46]*You did not anoint my head with oil, but she has anointed my feet with ointment.* [47]*Therefore I tell you, her sins, which are many, are forgiven, for she loved much; but he who is forgiven little, loves little."* [48]*And he said to her, "Your sins are forgiven."* [49]*Then those who were at table with him began to say among themselves, "Who is this, who even forgives sins?"* [50]*And he said to the woman, "Your faith has saved you; go in peace."*

The brief parable found in Luke 7:41, 42 is set in an important context. Simon, a Pharisee, had invited Jesus home to a meal. Scholars generally assume it was an after-service invitation on the Sabbath. It was a common practice to ask home for dinner the one who gave the scriptural interpretation in the Sabbath service. The seating custom was to recline on cushions around a low table with the participants' feet angled outward and their head resting on the bent elbow. Anyone approaching the guests would naturally come up behind the nearest eaters.

Verse 37 introduces the other central figure rather abruptly. "And behold, a woman of the city, who was a sinner." In this context the description "sinner" almost certainly means "prostitute." If it is true that the meal followed a Sabbath service in which Jesus had led out, the woman may well have heard His comments on that day's text. In any case, she must have known enough about Jesus' preaching to believe that God had forgiven her.

When the woman learned that Jesus was a guest at Simon's house, she entered bearing a long-necked flask of perfume. This was quite a brazen act, because women were not invited to such meals. The woman stood behind Jesus at His feet and wept. Her falling tears moistened His feet, much to her embarrassment. In spontaneous concern she let down her hair and used her tresses to towel His feet. Jewish women plaited their hair and held it up with a bandannalike covering. It was considered a disgraceful act for a woman to untie her hair in public. In fact, Jewish law listed loosing the hair before other men as grounds for divorce. It appears that letting the hair down and using it to dry a client's feet was a service of call girls (called *hetairai*, that is, "female companions") at male feasts.

Socially, then, the woman's act was indecent, shameless. With skills learned in her despicable trade, she next tenderly kissed Jesus' feet and anointed them with her expensive perfume. The Jews considered a harlot's money tainted, and no pious person would accept anything—not even a gift—from such a person. The woman's initial intrusion surprised the guests, but now her shameless display of gratitude and devotion disgusted them. Simon in particular was shocked at Jesus' acceptance of the prostitute's attentions.

Simon had thought that Jesus was a prophet, but he now doubted it. If He were a prophet, Simon mused, He would know what kind of woman this is. Equally, if He did know and still allowed her to touch Him, He is no true prophet.

But Simon's observations were wrong. Jesus knew who the woman was, yet He welcomed her action toward Him. For Jesus is more than a prophet; He is the Saviour. The woman perceived this and rejoiced. Simon did not, so he doubted even what he had thought.

The pouring of water for the guests' feet was a servant's task. Greeting someone with a kiss was reserved for relatives, children, or a friend returning from a long journey. Anointing with oil occurred only on festive occasions. The Pharisee saw nothing so extraordinary about Jesus' presence in his home, so he did not do any of these things to Jesus. The prostitute knew otherwise. Moved by the deepest gratitude, she felt compelled to show her devotion with an uninhibited display. The parable Jesus related to Simon cleared the woman of Simon's condemnation and gently suggested that even the pious host was not beyond reproach.

Two different debtors owed a creditor sums of money. One owed 50 denarii; the other, 500. When neither could repay him, the moneylender canceled both debts. "Which of them," Jesus asked Simon, "will love him more?" (verse 42). Confronted by Jesus' question, Simon had to give an answer that passed sentence on himself. (Compare chap. 10:36.) The Pharisee could not reply that the man whose 50 denarii debt was remitted would be more grateful, for Simon would lose credibility. He was obliged to admit that the debtor who received the greater remission would love his benefactor the more (chap. 7:43). His pronouncement cleared the woman's conduct, for he himself had thus declared that her lavish display indicated a correspondingly large remission. Jesus' story gently rebuked Simon for having a limited appreciation of his own need for forgiveness.

Some commentators, especially Catholic scholars, interpret verse 47 to mean that the woman's sins were forgiven because she loved much. A number of factors prove that the reverse is true. First, it is clear that the woman entered Simon's house already overcome with gratitude prior to the demonstration of her love. Second, the last part of verse 47 makes forgiveness the cause of love: "He who is forgiven little, loves little." Jesus' concluding remark also indicates this: "Your faith has saved you" (verse 50). Third, and most important, the whole point of the parable is that great love is the result of, not the cause of, great forgiveness.

How, then, should the clause "for she loved much" (verse 47) be understood? It must be attached to the verb *to tell* rather than the verb *to forgive*. The verse can be translated this way: "Therefore I tell you—because she loved much—her sins, which are many, have been forgiven by God." The woman's love gave Jesus grounds for declaring to Simon that God had forgiven her. The angry glances of Simon and his guests had intimidated the woman, and her self-confidence had wavered. Therefore Jesus turned to her and said assuringly, "Your sins are forgiven" (verse 48). Ignoring the incredulous murmurs of the others, He continued, "Your faith has saved you; go in peace" (verse 50).

The prostitute's love demonstrated her acceptance of God's prior forgiveness. Her great love did not *cause* God's forgiveness, but *testified* to it. *The New English Bible* renders verse 47 excellently: "And so, I tell you, her great love proves that her many sins have been forgiven." The passive voice is a Jewish circumlocution for the name God, and thus the verse can be rendered as "have been forgiven by God." Paul caught the truth of this parable and wrote, "Do you not know that God's kindness is meant to lead you to repentance?" (Rom. 2:4). For God showed His love for us in that Christ died for us before we believed, even while we were yet sinners (chap. 5:8).

CHAPTER 2

The Good Samaritan

Luke 10:25-37

25 And behold, a lawyer stood up to put him to the test, saying, "Teacher, what shall I do to inherit eternal life?" 26He said to him, "What is written in the law? How do you read?" 27And he answered, "You shall love the Lord your God with all your heart, and with all your soul, and with all your strength, and with all your mind; and your neighbor as yourself." 28And he said to him, "You have answered right; do this, and you will live." 29But he, desiring to justify himself, said to Jesus, "And who is my neighbor?" 30Jesus replied, "A man was going down from Jerusalem to Jericho, and he fell among robbers, who stripped him and beat him, and departed, leaving him half dead. 31Now by chance a priest was going down that road; and when he saw him he passed by on the other side. 32So likewise a Levite, when he came to the place and saw him, passed by on the other side. 33But a Samaritan, as he journeyed, came to where he was; and when he saw him, he had compassion, 34and went to him and bound up his wounds, pouring on oil and wine; then he set him on his own beast and brought him to an inn, and took care of him. ³⁵*And the next day he took out two denarii and gave them to the innkeeper, saying, 'Take care of him; and whatever more you spend, I will repay you when I come back.'* ³⁶*Which of these three, do you think, proved neighbor to the man who fell among the robbers?"* ³⁷*He said, "The one who showed mercy on him." And Jesus said to him, "Go and do likewise."*

For modern Christians the noun *Samaritan* automatically attracts the adjective *good* to it. The term *Samaritan* has become synonymous today with being a good neighbor and helping the needy. No doubt this is why Loma Linda University Medical Center in California placed a sculpture of the Samaritan on its lawn. But the last thing that Jews of Jesus' day would have associated with the word *Samaritan* was the adjective *good*. An intense and mutual hatred existed between Jews and Samaritans in the first century. The bitter feud between them was basically a religious quarrel about priestly succession and the correct place of worship. Hence hatred raged especially fierce between the Jewish priestly class and the Samaritans. We must keep in mind this religious and national hostility when reading Jesus' parable.

The parable of the good Samaritan is a segment in a dialogue between Jesus and a Jewish lawyer (that is, an expert in Jewish religious law). The dialogue falls into two parts, with balanced question and counterquestion.

THE GOOD SAMARITAN

PART ONE

Lawyer's Question: "What shall I do to inherit eternal life?" (verse 25).

Jesus' Counterquestion: "What is written in the law? How do you read?" (verse 26; that is, "What do you think it means?").

Lawyer's Answer: "You shall love the Lord your God . . . and your neighbor" (verse 27).

Jesus' Answer/Exhortation: "Do this, and you will live" (verse 28).

PART TWO

Lawyer's Question: "Who is my neighbor?" (verse 29).

Jesus' Counterquestion: "Which of these three . . . proved neighbor?" (verse 36).

Lawyer's Answer: "The one who showed mercy" (verse 37).

Jesus' Answer/Exhortation: "Go and do likewise" (verse 37).*

The parable of the good Samaritan prepared for Jesus' counterquestion in the second part of the dialogue and gave His question its bite.

The exchange between Jesus and the lawyer opened with the latter asking a simple test question (verse 25). No doubt he expected the stock answer, which he himself already knew (verse 27). Such an answer from Jesus would have given the lawyer the opportunity to try to humiliate the

---

* Drawn from K. E. Bailey, *Poet and Peasant* (Grand Rapids: Eerdmans, 1976), p. 74.

Galilean Layman with his clever objection "And who is my neighbor?" (verse 29). Jesus' counter-question, however, made the lawyer's ploy impossible. Since he was an expert, the lawyer had to give the well-known answer (verse 27) or lose face. In order to regain prestige before the crowd for having asked a question that he himself answered, the lawyer entered into a second exchange. The lawyer was now obliged, however, to ask his query as a genuine inquiry, and not as a clever objection intended to embarrass the provincial Teacher (verse 29). The parable of the good Samaritan formed a crucial part of Jesus' answer.

Why did the lawyer ask the question "Who is my neighbor?" It was a topic frequently debated by the Jewish teachers. What the lawyer wished to know was how far he must extend the category *neighbor.* Clearly excluded were prostitutes, slaves, gamblers, usurers, pigeon trainers (because of their association with gambling), herdsmen (because they were notoriously dishonest), tax collectors, and especially Samaritans. The lawyer required Jesus to give him a standard by which he could readily discriminate between those whom he should treat as friends and those whom he need not.

Surprisingly, Jesus did not answer the lawyer's question directly. Instead, He told a story about someone who acted as the neighbor (see verse 36). But the lawyer wanted to know whom he must treat as a neighbor (verse 29). The lawyer could walk away agreeing that he must show mercy as the Samaritan had done, but still muttering, "Yes, but to whom? That's my question." However, the lawyer's question verbally can mean "Who is neighbor to me?" The lawyer obviously did not have this in mind, but that is how Jesus answered it.

By answering the question with this meaning ("Who is neighbor to me?" instead of "To whom am I to be neighbor?"), Jesus forced the smug lawyer to identify with the wounded Jew in the parable. In this way the lawyer found himself, as it were, beaten up and bleeding alongside the Jericho road. It was no longer a question of who qualified for his help, but who would help him. Such a twist characterizes a number of Jesus' stories.

The lawyer quoted Leviticus 19:18 ("You shall love your neighbor as yourself") as the answer to his own initial interrogation. Jesus approved his reply. But the parable of the good Samaritan gave this correct answer a depth unsuspected by the lawyer. The Leviticus command should not be expanded to mean "You shall love your neighbor as you love yourself," but "You shall love your neighbor *as though* loving yourself." The love command does not simply urge the sharing of one's self-love with another. Rather, it demands radically putting oneself in the other's place before dealing with him.

The average layman—and this included the lawyer—in Jesus' day had a low opinion of the upper-class Temple priests. The indifference of the priest and Levite in passing by the wounded Jew would not have startled the scribes and Pharisees (usually pious laymen). But the compassion of a hated Samaritan would have been an unbearable shock. Many Jews would have preferred to be left half dead by the road than be tended by a Samaritan. A modern parallel to this bitterness would be to tell a Northern Irish Presbyterian congregation about an Anglican clergyman and a Methodist minister who passed by a wounded Irish Presbyterian. And then contrast this with a southern Irish Catholic priest who stopped to help.

Jesus enforced the depth of the Samaritan's compassion by relating details of his help to the wounded Jew. The Samaritan cleansed the wounds with wine. He soothed them with oil and bandaged them. He placed the injured man on his beast of burden and took him to an inn. There he personally cared for the Jew until the next day. Prior to his departure he made provision for several more days of care and gave his guarantee to pay any costs that exceeded that amount.

Jesus did not tell a parable of a Jew who helped a Samaritan and then exhort the lawyer to do likewise. Instead, He had the traditional enemy help the Jew, and then He gave His admonition. To receive love from an "inferior" enemy bites harder than being charitable to our foes. "Who was neighbor?" Jesus searchingly inquired. But the lawyer could not say the despised word *Samaritan*, so he used a circumlocution, "The one who showed mercy on him" (verse 37). "Having yourself," Jesus inferred, "been so helped, go and do likewise."

Never again could "Love your neighbor" carry the corollary "Hate your enemy" (Matt. 5:43). Jesus declared that the love command included enemies. The parable thrusts home Jesus' basic teaching. The Samaritan loved one who did not love him (see Luke 6:32). He did good without any thought of personal benefit (see verses 33, 34). He lent, expecting nothing in return (see verse 35). This is what Jesus meant when He challenged His hearers with the declaration "Love your enemies" (verses 27, 35).

The self-confident lawyer made no protest that Jesus had not really answered his question. His original question, "What shall I do to inherit eternal life" (verse 25) had received an unequivocal reply, "Show mercy on your enemy as the Samaritan did" (verse 37). Furthermore, Jesus did not leave him worrying about whom he should include in his list of neighbors. No. Jesus' parable left him musing about what *he* would do if *he* met a wounded Samaritan.

The Friend at Midnight

Luke 11:5-13

5 And he said to them, "Which of you who has a friend will go to him at midnight and say to him, 'Friend, lend me three loaves; ⁶for a friend of mine has arrived on a journey, and I have nothing to set before him'; ⁷and he will answer from within, 'Do not bother me; the door is now shut, and my children are with me in bed; I cannot get up and give you anything'? ⁸I tell you, though he will not get up and give him anything because he is his friend, yet because of his importunity he will rise and give him whatever he needs. ⁹And I tell you, Ask, and it will be given you; seek, and you will find; knock, and it will be opened to you. ¹⁰For every one who asks receives, and he who seeks finds, and to him who knocks it will be opened. ¹¹What father among you, if his son asks for a fish, will instead of a fish give him a serpent; ¹²or if he asks for an egg, will give him a scorpion? ¹³If you then, who are evil, know how to give good gifts to your children, how much more will the heavenly Father give the Holy Spirit to those who ask him!"

The boys' council had met, lots had been cast, and it had fallen upon a certain emaciated waif to confront the master who dispensed the gruel. That evening—egged on by the winks and nudges of his table companions (to say nothing of his own gnawing hunger)—Oliver tremblingly advanced to the master and politely asked, "Please, sir, I want some more."

After a prolonged silence, the rotund master gasped, "What!"

So Oliver repeated his demand—and received a clout with the ladle for his trouble.

The beadle (a church official) was summoned. When he learned of Oliver's impertinent demand, he rushed to the governing committee and announced that Oliver had asked for more. Horrified looks clouded the board members' faces. And the chairman, Mr. Limbkins, exclaimed, "For more!"

To which the beadle replied disbelievingly, "He did, sir?"

Is praying to God a fearsome act akin to Oliver's nervous procession past the pinched faces of his fellow orphans? Is God like the fat master whom Oliver confronted with his unheard-of request? Do we, like Queen Esther, have to make elaborate preparations before we enter the throne room of the King? Must we fast and rehearse our words in an attempt to find the correct formula? Jesus related a parable that gives us a clear answer.

In it He invited His Eastern audience to imagine a scene that in their culture was inconceivable. "Can you imagine," He asked His listeners, "a situation in which you went to a friend late at night to borrow some bread that you needed to entertain an unexpected guest, only to have your friend complain and grumble about your request? In light of the importance placed on hospitality in first-century Palestine, no hearer of Jesus' query could imagine such a grudging response.

A number of times Jesus began a parable or saying with the query "Who among you . . . ?" (for example, see Matt. 6:27; 12:11; Luke 11:11; 12:25; 14:5, 28; 15:4; 17:7). In each case the expected answer is "None of us would (would not)." Thus the same inquiry at the introduction of the parable of the friend at midnight (chap 11:5) also requires a negative response. None of Jesus' listeners could imagine a *friend* who would belligerently refuse a plea for help in a matter of hospitality, not even at the inconvenient hour of midnight.

The difficulties proffered by the man awakened by the nocturnal visitor pleading for help were merely the superficial grumbles of someone reluctant to supply the sought-for aid. The unexpected request for three loaves of bread was a nuisance, and he did not seize the occasion as an opportunity to assist a friend.

Instead, he complained that the door was locked and that he and his children were in bed. Any movement, he implied, in his dark, crowded one-room quarters (the usual size of a Palestinian house at the time) would cause a disturbance and no end of inconvenience. "Don't trouble me," he irritably murmured from within, "for under the circumstances it is quite impossible for me to get up."

The requested loaves of bread were about the

size of a modern bun, hence the comparison with a stone (Matt. 7:9). Each meal began with the breaking of the loaf, for a piece of bread served as the customary eating utensil. Bread, therefore, was as essential to an ancient Eastern meal as a knife and fork are today. The request, then, though coming at an awkward hour, was not trivial.

Jesus concluded that even if the scoundrel inside the house did not supply the requested loaves on account of his friendship with the caller, he would do so because of the midnight caller's audacity. The word translated "importunity" in Luke 11:8 does not mean "persistence" (a positive quality) but "shamelessness, impudence, audacity" (a negative quality). The caller at midnight does not offer an example of tenacity. Rather, it is the caller's somewhat shameless conduct in calling upon a friend in the middle of the night that verse 8 emphasizes.

Nevertheless, in spite of the dire circumstances, friendship should have met the caller's need. The wakened sleeper's whining excuses would have shocked an Eastern audience. The awakened man's initial refusal meant the failure of his friendship—a terrible offense. Since his friendship proved inadequate, the caller is left with brazenness alone with which to move the sleepy man into giving him the needed bread.

The midnight caller thus succeeded through his impudence rather than because of the expected response of friendship. This is in contrast to poor Oliver, whose impertinence was insufficient to move the custodians of the gruel. God, however, is not like the robust master who presided over the gruel vat, or like the Persian despot whom Queen Esther faced. Neither does He resemble the grumbling "friend" upon whom the caller at midnight depended. "The selfish neighbor . . . does not represent the character of God. The lesson is drawn, not by comparison, but by contrast."— *Christ's Object Lessons,* p. 141.

A selfish man will grant an urgent request so as to be rid of the one whose brazenness has annoyingly disturbed his rest (*ibid.*). But God is not like a selfish man. We need only ask and God will give, for He is the giving God. Seek and you will find, for He is the seeking God. Knock and He will open, for He is the open God. (See verses 9, 10.) If earthly fathers, who are evil, generally give good gifts to their children, "how much more will the heavenly Father give . . . to those who ask him!" (verse 13).

Prayer, then, does not badger God into action. It is not a weapon with which to overcome His supposed reluctance. Prayer is the conversation of trust, the communion of friends. Some think that because God knows everything, we should limit prayer to praise and so abandon intercessory and petitionary prayer. Of course, we do not pray to inform an ignorant God or to remind a forgetful God. In prayer we identify with God's purposes, and thus His concerns become our concerns. Indeed, Jesus taught that God's foreknowledge is an assumption of prayer (Matt. 6:8). Since He knows our needs before we ask, our prayers do not inform or coerce Him, but rather express our confidence in Him. The Christian, then, prays to a good Friend, not a sluggish grumbler. A Friend who anticipates our needs and is never annoyed at our approach, not even at an awkward hour like midnight.

Paul affirmed Jesus' teaching concerning the God to whom Christians pray, but with one expansion. Paul emphasized the death of Christ for us—the "inexpressible gift" (2 Cor. 9:15)—as the supreme guarantee that God is the great giver. "He who did not spare his own Son but gave him up for us all, will he not also give us all things with him?" (Rom. 8:32). The Christian does not continue in prayer in order to assail with a verbal barrage some hardened God. In Jesus' name he knows that he addresses "the Father of mercies and God of all comfort" (2 Cor. 1:3).

CHAPTER 4

The Parable of the Waster Son and His Brother

PART 1: THE PRODIGAL BROTHER

Luke 15:11-24

11 And he said, "There was a man who had two sons; [12]and the younger of them said to his father, 'Father, give me the share of property that falls to me.' And he divided his living between them. [13]Not many days later, the younger son gathered all he had and took his journey into a far country, and there he squandered his property in loose living. [14]And when he had spent everything, a great famine arose in that country, and he began to be in want. [15]So he went and joined himself to one of the citizens of that country, who sent him into his fields to feed swine. [16]And he would gladly have fed on the pods that the swine ate; and no one gave him anything. [17]But when he came to himself he said, 'How many of my father's hired servants have bread enough and to spare, but I perish here with hunger! [18]I will arise and go to my father, and I will say to him, "Father, I have sinned against heaven and before you; [19]I am no longer worthy to be called your son; treat me as one of your hired servants."' [20]And he arose and came to his father. But while he was yet at a

distance, his father saw him and had compassion, and ran and embraced him and kissed him. ²¹And the son said to him, 'Father, I have sinned against heaven and before you; I am no longer worthy to be called your son.' ²²But the father said to his servants, 'Bring quickly the best robe, and put it on him; and put a ring on his hand, and shoes on his feet; ²³and bring the fatted calf and kill it, and let us eat and make merry; ²⁴for this my son was dead, and is alive again; he was lost, and is found.' And they began to make merry."

The longest, the best known, most loved, most quoted, but least understood parable of Jesus is the one about the prodigal son. The traditional title, the average sermon, and the majority of paintings of this parable stop at verse 24. For most people the return of the prodigal, or waster, son constitutes the climax of this story. Indeed, some prefer to ignore the section dealing with the elder brother because they feel uncomfortable with the younger son's apparently better treatment.

The father, who is the central figure in the parable, was anything but typical. Most fathers, as A. M. Hunter suggests, would kill the prodigal rather than the fatted calf (*The Parables Then and Now*, p. 60). Jesus' Jewish contemporaries would have applauded a story about a father who demanded repentance and positive proof of amendment before receiving back a dissolute son. Repentance lay at the very heart of Pharisaism. It preceded God's forgiveness and involved a period of probation and separation to prove its genuineness.

Jesus associated and ate with sinners (verses 1,

2). He accepted them before they showed any sign of repentance or reformation. The sincerely religious were offended at such conduct by a holy teacher. The parable of the prodigal son is one of a trio that Jesus gave in His defense.

In the preceding parables of the lost sheep and the lost coin, Jesus emphasized the divine initiative in finding the lost. God is like a woman down on hands and knees with lighted lamp seeking her own. Or He is like a shepherd trudging the hills and listening for the bleat of the missing lamb. Jesus declared that God does not wait for human repentance or reformation before extending His mercy. He lavishly proffers His acceptance prior to any moral transformation. Repentance thus *accepts* but *does not cause* the divine remission. This was directly opposite to the Pharisees' view.

"But in the parable of the lost sheep, Christ teaches that salvation does not come through our seeking after God but through God's seeking after us. . . . We do not repent in order that God may love us, but He reveals to us His love in order that we may repent."—*Christ's Object Lessons*, p. 189. But does not the prodigal son differ from the lost sheep and the lost coin? He came to his senses (verse 17). He returned painfully to the family estate (verse 20). He changed his original "Give me" (verse 12) to "Treat me" (verse 19). Surely, this was a repentance that preceded acceptance? Further study of the parable is required before accepting this position.

Emigration commonly occurs when an agrarian economy, like first-century Palestine, experiences overcrowding. In Jesus' time there were about half a million Jews in Palestine, compared with 4 million who lived outside Palestine. It was not, therefore, unusual for a son to want to leave the family farm and seek his fortune in the world of the Gentiles. However, the request for one's share of the estate was not normal. Eastern culture considered such a request an insult to the father. It virtually expressed the son's wish for the father's immediate death. It transgressed the fifth commandment and indicated that the son was more concerned about the father's property than for his father.

Ancient parents, as today, felt reluctant to hand over their property before they died. They feared that their children might leave them destitute in their old age. Jesus' Jewish audience would, therefore, have expected the father angrily to refuse his son's demand. But, as has been said, this father was not typical. He generously granted the younger son his share of the property. He protected the older brother's portion by gifting it to him also (note verse 12, "between *them*"). This procedure left the father in control of the estate's produce, but it secured the terms of the disposal of the property after his death.

The father had, of course, given the younger son immediate possession of his share. Generally this would have been one third of the estate, though perhaps under the extraordinary circumstances it was less. Within days the younger son had sold his share for ready cash (verse 13, N.E.B.). This almost certainly involved the sale of part of the property. Now with his inheritance at his disposal, the young ne'er-do-well set off to seek his fortune in the prosperous commercial world of the Gentiles. The attractions there proved irresistible. He lived recklessly and squandered his inheritance in riotous living.

That many a young man's inherited fortune was consumed on wine, women, and song is well attested in the ancient sources. Thus the young man's sin was by no means unique. Though it was common, the ancient sages universally condemned such folly. Judaism, however, condemned not only the dissipated lifestyle but even more the thoughtless loss of the means to support the father in his old age. Sons were expected to assist financially their aged parents in cases of necessity.

To make matters worse, a famine hit the Gentile country. Destitute and hungry, the young Jew took a job with a Gentile as a swineherd. The young fool's wild life now became a clear matter of apostasy. He had a Gentile employer. His occupation as a swineherd was accursed according to Jewish law. Sabbath observance, the maintenance of ritual purity, and adherence to the details of the Jewish law were all impossible. Jesus obviously alluded here in this parable to the Jewish tax collectors, who also had polluted themselves by working for the Gentiles.

The herding job not only was degrading but also, in the famine conditions, provided the barest subsistence. The young man would gladly have made up for his lack of sufficient food by supplementing his diet with the pigs' food (carob husks). But it was exclusively for the pigs and not to be shared with the foreign hireling—"no one gave him anything [of the pigs' feed]" (verse 16).

There is a fourth century A.D. Jewish saying that

when an Israelite is reduced to carob pods, he repents. The prodigal was no exception. He saw things clearly now for the first time. Home was not such a bad place after all. He knew he had lost the status of a son, but even as a day laborer, home was home. So he headed back.

We should not overpraise the young man's coming to his senses (verse 17). It was a pragmatic perception brought about by dire necessity. His prepared speech confessed his sin and asked for a chance to redeem himself by working as a hired hand (verses 18, 19). He neither expected nor desired any preferential treatment, just the opportunity to prove his changed life by working for a daily wage. Indeed, such workers usually slept off the farm.

In later Judaism, the rabbis taught that God and man cooperate in repentance. For every step we take toward God in repentance, God takes one toward us. Repentance was central to Jewish religion. Provided it was sincere and involved separations and a determination to avoid all further sin, it wrought atonement. We noted earlier that the prodigal's repentance seemed to precede the father's forgiveness. This is because the prodigal son behaved according to Judaism's concept of repentance. But the father's conduct revealed different principles.

As the waster neared the end of his journey, news of his approach preceded him. On his entering the village, small boys gathered about him, and soon a crowd assembled. Their faces, of course, would not have expressed welcome. The villagers could not have anticipated the next scene in the dramatic arrival.

Even when aged Orientals were in a hurry, it was beneath their dignity to run. The father's haste was humbling in the eyes of the accompanying household slaves and the gathered villagers. But his joy could not heed the cultural etiquette (see verse 20). He kissed his son and embraced him around the neck. By doing so, he prevented his son from kneeling in a posture of subservience. The kiss signified oneness. The whole of the father's action and visible compassion declared the prodigal's acceptance as a son. The father's snapped orders to the household slaves informed them that they were to respect the returned prodigal as his son. The command to fetch quickly the best robe, a ring (a sign of authority), and shoes (a freeman's luxury) and to prepare for a banquet told the uncertain servants and the incredulous crowd that he had forgiven and reinstated his son.

The father's dramatic display prevented the son from finishing his nicely rehearsed speech. He had just declared that he was not worthy to be called a son (verse 21), and was about to make his climactic request to be treated as a hired hand, when the father's action interrupted him (verse 22). All talk of being a day laborer was banished by the challenge of the gracious offer of full sonship. The son's traditional idea of repentance (repentance procures reconciliation) was shattered by the father's lavish action of forgiveness (repentance accepts reconciliation). "Repentance finally turns out to be the capacity to forego [sic] pride and accept graciousness."—Dan O. Via, Jr., *The Parables*, p. 171.

The imagery is one that was precious to Paul. "So through God [the Father's initiative] you are no longer a slave but a son, and if a son then an heir" (Gal. 4:7). But some protest at this. Hence Jesus' parable continues, for He mainly addressed it to these objectors. Part 2, which follows, deals not with an appendix, as some think, but with the climax of the parable.

CHAPTER 5

The Parable of the Waster Son and His Brother

PART 2: THE OLDER BROTHER

Luke 15:25-32

25 "Now his elder son was in the field; and as he came and drew near to the house, he heard music and dancing. ²⁶And he called one of the servants and asked what this meant. ²⁷And he said to him, 'Your brother has come, and your father has killed the fatted calf, because he has received him safe and sound.' ²⁸But he was angry and refused to go in. His father came out and entreated him, ²⁹but he answered his father, 'Lo, these many years I have served you, and I never disobeyed your command; yet you never gave me a kid, that I might make merry with my friends. ³⁰But when this son of yours came, who has devoured your living with harlots, you killed for him the fatted calf!' ³¹And he said to him, 'Son, you are always with me, and all that is mine is yours. ³²It was fitting to make merry and be glad, for this your brother was dead, and is alive; he was lost, and is found.' "

The almost identical conclusion in verses 24 and 32—"For this your brother ["my son," verse 24] was dead, and is alive; he was lost, and is found"—indicates the natural division of the parable into two parts. In the second section, Jesus is exposing the attitude of the Pharisees (verses 25-32). His teaching that divine mercy is spontaneous, free, and lavish offended them. His attitude in accepting sinners before reformation and without probation they found especially objectionable. The older brother expressed their feelings.

The experience of the older brother partially parallels that of the younger. He too was in a field (cf. verses 15 and 25). Like the prodigal, he approached the house and met with signs of joy (cf. verses 20 and 25). But from here on he showed a different spirit. He became suspicious when he heard the music and dancing, so he called a passing servant and asked what was going on. The servant told him that his brother had returned and that his father was celebrating the event with a banquet (verse 27). This information angered the older brother, and he refused to enter the house to join in the festivities (verse 28).

The older brother's behavior severely slighted the father, and his pouting outside soon became known. The music died out; the dancing stopped. The hushed guests awaited the expected violent parental reaction. However, for the second time that day the father humbled himself and went out to his son (verse 28). He went outside not to deliver the anticipated rebuke, but to plead.

The older brother stated his complaint in bitter terms, and probably in the guests' hearing: "Lo, these many years I have served you, and I never disobeyed your command; yet you never gave me a kid, that I might make merry with my friends" (verse 29). This outburst brought the father's entreaty to a sudden halt.

"I never disobeyed." Ironically, the older son transgressed this boast in the very process of making it. His insolent protest flew in the face of the fifth commandment, the very one that the prodigal had violated. Also, like the prodigal, he showed more concern for the father's property than for the father. The father assured him that the younger son's return did not threaten his share: "All that is mine is yours" (verse 31). This assurance reminded the belligerent older son that all the father's possessions were his also for the asking. Apparently he yearned for the day when he did not have to ask. He was impatient, as the prodigal had been, for the father's death. The father's words "you are always with me" (verse 31) expressed the older son's problem, not his joy.

The older brother considered himself a righteous person who needed no repentance (see verse 7). In his eyes the father rewarded wasters and deprived the diligent of their just reward. It was not the father's generosity that upset him, but that a waster should be the recipient of it. As T. W. Manson delightfully puts it: "It is the veal that sticks in his gullet, not the goat's flesh."—*The Sayings of Jesus*, p. 290.

Each of the three parables in Luke 15 concludes with an invitation to others to rejoice with the finder who had successfully recovered the lost possession (verses 6, 9, 23, 24, 32). Through these stories Jesus defended His own eating with sinners. His presence at their table brought God's forgiveness and made the meal a celebration of acceptance. He invited the Pharisees to participate in the Finder's joy.

Many ask at this point, "If God extends His mercy so freely to sinners, why the cross? Where is there any mention of atonement or incarnation?" The parable of the prodigal son refers to the spontaneity of forgiveness, not the cost. Nevertheless, the humiliation of the father is the essence of the atonement. His going out to his prodigal son and his angry son involved cost and shame. He confronted insult with love, and met pride with humility. The phrases "emptied himself," "humbled himself," and "despising the shame" (Phil. 2:7, 8; Heb. 12:2) describe the father's conduct in the parable, as well as the atonement.

In Ephesians 2:4-22 Paul recaptured the gospel message of the parable of the waster son and his brother and reapplied it to his concern for the reconciliation of Jew and Gentile. Paul spoke of the Gentiles as "far off" (verses 13, 17), and the Jews as "near" (verse 17). The cross, he said, has united Jew and Gentile, and through Christ they both have access to the Father (verse 18). Gentiles are now "members of the household of God" (verse 19). Those who were once dead have now been made alive by God's grace and mercy (verses 5-8). Paul paraphrases the language of the parable of the prodigal son (Luke 15:32). He, at least, saw no conflict between the atonement and the message of Jesus' parable.

So despite a common misconception, the older brother was not ill-treated, and the younger was not made a favorite. The same fatherly love

45

extended sonship to both, "for there is no distinction between Jew and Greek; the same Lord is Lord of all and bestows his riches upon all who call upon him" (Rom. 10:12). "God has consigned all men to disobedience, that he may have mercy upon all" (chap. 11:32).

Jesus does not tell us how either brother ultimately responded. The younger brother is last seen feasting inside the house, and the older brother remains outside fuming. "For the parable was still enacting, and it rested with His hearers to determine what the outcome should be."—*Christ's Object Lessons*, p. 209. Moreover, because the challenge of this parable continues to require a response whether we identify with the waster son or his brother, the parable is still not finished.

CHAPTER 6

The Unjust Steward

Luke 16:1-9

1 And he told them a parable, to the effect that they ought . . . He also said to the disciples "There was a rich man who had a steward, and charges were brought to him that this man was wasting his goods. ²And he called him and said to him, 'What is this that I hear about you? Turn in the account of your stewardship, for you can no longer be steward.' ³And the steward said to himself, 'What shall I do, since my master is taking the stewardship away from me? I am not strong enough to dig, and I am ashamed to beg. ⁴I have decided what to do, so that people may receive me into their houses when I am put out of the stewardship.' ⁵So, summoning his master's debtors one by one, he said to the first, 'How much do you owe my master?' ⁶He said, 'A hundred measures of oil.' And he said to him, 'Take your bill, and sit down quickly and write fifty.' ⁷Then he said to another, 'And how much do you owe?' He said, 'A hundred measures of wheat.' He said to him, 'Take your bill, and write eighty.' ⁸The master commended the dishonest steward for his shrewdness; for the sons of this world are more shrewd in dealing with their own generation than the sons of light. ⁹And I tell you, make friends for yourselves by means of unrighteous mammon, so that when it fails they may receive you into the eternal habitations."

Who commended the unjust steward? Some scholars think that the "master," or "lord" (K.J.V.), in verse 8 refers to Jesus. Verse 8 would then give Jesus' own comment on the parable. Luke's Gospel has several instances in which Jesus does this. Luke 12:42a and 18:6 are examples where "Lord" refers to Jesus and His comment on the preceding parable. However, there are other occasions in Luke where "lord" (K.J.V.) refers to the master in the parable (cf. chaps. 12:37, 42b; 14:23). If Luke 16:8 were a comment by Jesus, the parable would abruptly end in verse 7. For this reason it is best to take verse 8 as a reference to the same master mentioned in verses 3 and 5. Verse 8 is then part of the parable and not, as some think, Jesus' comment on it.

This position raises a problem with plausibility. Is it likely that the master would praise the scoundrel who had cheated him? Some commentators have avoided the difficulty of this question by arguing that the master was not ripped off. They arrive at this position in one of two ways: either by suggesting that the master himself was advantaged by the steward's dubious transactions or by proposing that the steward simply relinquished his personal commission. Both of these suggestions are unsatisfactory. There is no hint of the former in the parable, and the latter would hardly merit calling the steward unjust. For a better solution we must examine the parable in more detail.

The rich man mentioned at the beginning of the parable owned an estate. Such wealthy landholders commonly leased out their land for a set rent. The steward (verse 1) was the landowner's estate manager or agent. He was the master's legal representative in all his business dealings with the lessees. The steward earned a fixed salary, not a commission. The suggestion that he simply forwent his own legitimate cut is, therefore, culturally indefensible. In his position he no doubt received numerous favors, but these were strictly off the record.

Someone brought charges against the manager, accusing him of squandering the master's goods. The steward's later reaction indicates that his character rather than his ability was probably the problem. The estate owner took immediate steps to deal with the situation. He ordered his steward forthwith to turn in the account books (verse 2). During the investigation of the ledgers, he was deprived of his office.

Since the charges were true, he knew full well the outcome of the audit. His future looked grim as he contemplated the alternatives. His sedentary tasks had not equipped him for hard manual labor. Begging was too humiliating even to consider. Faced with such dreadful future prospects, he decided on a desperate plan of action.

He summoned his master's debtors—the lease-holders who paid an agreed rent in produce. Apparently they had not yet learned that the steward was out of office and under scrutiny. In his capacity as business manager, he ordered the lessees to write new contracts very much in their favor.

The two discounts—fifty measures of oil and twenty of wheat—had the same value. Each cut was worth about one and a half year's average wage. Too large for a commission. Besides, the steward would hardly exchange such a vast sum, if it were his own, for some possible but not certain future hospitality. Clearly the accounts that the steward so generously reduced were the master's. It cost the manager nothing to obligate his master's debtors to himself. It would, of course, be impossible for the master to dishonor the new contracts. Such a reversal of his perceived generosity would have brought shame upon himself, for the steward had acted in his name. It is in this context that we must perceive the master's praise of the unjust steward.

The master did not praise the business manager for swindling him. For that and other misdemeanors he had dismissed him. But he did grudgingly respect the fellow's ingenuity in a crisis. The steward dealt with the immediate emergency in such a way as to secure future blessings. Such coolheadedness (though not the dishonesty) in a crisis is commendable and, according to Jesus, worthy of emulation by the sons of light (see verse 8). The coming of Jesus brought a time of crisis (chap. 12:49-59). The seriousness of the situation required prudent discernment of the times and appropriate conduct to assure a prosperous future (see chap. 13:1-5).

The terms *they* and *friends* in Luke 16:9 have

no allegorical reference to God and the angels or the poor. Jesus is using generalized language that reflects the speech of the parable. It is an exhortation to His disciples (verse 1) "Be ready for a welcome at the end by being generous in your life now, for the end is at hand." Jesus taught that the resources of this life were already passing away. An eternal dwelling could be secured only by a wise use of those things that would fail. Luke 12:33, 34 makes it clear, as does chapter 16:9, that this included money. Though, of course, "unrighteous mammon" is only an example and not the totality of discipleship (see chap. 14:33).

Jesus' parable does not teach that one may buy one's way into future glory. The preceding parables of Luke 15 should prevent any such misconception. However, Jesus constantly taught that the crisis which the presence of God's generosity in Himself brought (chap. 7:20-23; 11:20) demands a radical generosity in His disciples. To affirm God's generosity while denying the other, He said, was impossible. This tangible response is indispensable if one wills and desires to enter the abode of the blessed (chaps. 12:21; 16:19-31). Let "those who deal with the world [be] as though they had no dealings with it. For the form of this world is passing away" (1 Cor. 7:31).

CHAPTER 7

The Unjust Judge

Luke 18:1-8

1 And he told them a parable, to the effect that they ought always to pray and not lose heart. ²He said, "In a certain city there was a judge who neither feared God nor regarded man; ³and there was a widow in that city who kept coming to him and saying, 'Vindicate me against my adversary.' ⁴For a while he refused; but afterward he said to himself, 'Though I neither fear God nor regard man, ⁵yet because this widow bothers me, I will vindicate her, or she will wear me out by her continual coming.' " ⁶And the lord said, "Hear what the unrighteous judge says. ⁷And will not God vindicate his elect, who cry to him day and night? Will he delay long over them? ⁸I tell you, he will vindicate them speedily. Nevertheless, when the Son of man comes, will he find faith on earth?"

The community to which Luke wrote had begun to wonder why Christ had not yet returned (see Luke 12:35-48). Their prayers for God's intervention and final deliverance had started to falter. In the parable of the friend at midnight, Jesus taught that God would not, like some human friend, fail to honor His friendship. No, God could be relied upon as a true friend. Jesus thus grounded prayer in God's goodness, and no delay in the Advent could affect this basic reason—the faithfulness of God—for praying.

The present parable, like the one about the unresponsive friend, contrasts the attitude of the unjust judge with the character of God. "Christ here draws a sharp contrast between the unjust judge and God."—*Christ's Object Lessons*, p. 165. Neither parable teaches that persistence is the essence of prayer. It is true that both the awakened friend and the unjust judge protested that their callers caused them no end of bother (chaps. 11:7; 18:5). But this is part of the contrast, not a model to follow. Each of these parables is really Jesus' comment on His observation that if evil people (like a belligerent "friend" or a corrupt judge) know how to give good gifts, how much more God will give us the very best (chap. 11:13).

When Christians pray they are not to emulate either the impudence of the caller at midnight or the badgering tactics of the widow. Since God is not like a grumbling, half-asleep householder or an unjust judge, Christians should not approach Him in the spirit of the audacious midnight caller or the pestering widow.

Jesus certainly taught believers to continue in prayer. But this continuance was to express their trust in the faithfulness of God. It was not a device to overcome God's supposed indifference. We must not imagine that the petitioner has a greater social concern or deeper evangelistic zeal than the Petitioned. Prayer shares with God concerns and hopes that He has first given. In prayer the Christian is not informing God or instructing Him, but communing with Him. And God is a good listener.

A widow was probably the most socially vulnerable person in the ancient world. The Old Testament throughout depicts her as a supreme example of the innocent and powerless individual who is ever threatened by the oppression of the greedy and powerful. (See Deut. 10:18; 24:17; 27:19; Isa. 1:17; 10:2.) As such, widows should have had priority among those who were especially the objects of the judges' protection. The judge in this parable is not described in terms to encourage anyone to imagine that he glorified his office. Jesus says that the judge neither feared God nor showed any concern about what people thought of him (Luke 18:2). He was not likely to care twopence for any destitute widow.

In Jewish and Greek society, women did not as a rule have direct access to the courts. Generally a male family member who acted as their advocate had to represent them. In the context of this parable it would appear that the widow had no male family representative. Without male protection, she could easily be defrauded of whatever assets she possessed. Then, because she possessed no bribe money and no male guardian, it would be difficult for her to gain legal redress.

Desperate situations require desperate measures. The widow ignored social custom and kept on going to the corrupt judge to confront him continuously with her plea for justice. " ' "Vindicate me against my adversary," ' " she said (verse 3). She used legal language. Her words demanded that the judge make sure that she obtained her rights in a lawsuit. For a long time he paid no attention to her insistent request. Gradually, however, her regular appearance before him and her relentless demand for her rights began to irritate the unjust judge. He decided to vindicate her cause.

The judge's decision did not spring from any change in his character. His own thoughts indicated that he had no change of heart, for he still had no fear of God or any care about public opinion (verse 4). He took up the widow's case only because he wanted to be rid of her. He complained that she was a nuisance, and he feared that her continual coming would finally wear him out. At the end of his patience, with no high motive, he took up the widow's cause in order to free himself of her.

"Now listen," Jesus admonishes, "to what this parable of the unjust judge means" (verse 6, paraphrase). If an unscrupulous judge is prepared to vindicate a widow selfishly to procure his own peace and quiet, how much greater is the assurance that the righteous God will vindicate His elect? The Greek form of this question in verse 7 expects a strong affirmative answer: Yes, God certainly will vindicate His people! Indeed, Jesus gives just such a positive reply in verse 8. God's goodness and faithfulness guarantee His vindication of His elect. But will the community have to wait a long time? Must they pester God with their earnest pleas to force Him to act? No, Jesus replies, He will act speedily.

The fact that the elect pray day and night to God does not conflict with Jesus' promise that God will intervene soon on their behalf. Praying day and night indicates the intensity of the prayer, not that it is protracted.

The last part of verse 7 is difficult. The R.S.V. translation is probably wrong: "Will he delay long over them?" Literally it reads, "And He is long-suffering toward them." The point seems to be that God is patient toward His praying people and stays their judgment in order to allow continued opportunity for belief. The last half of verse 7 is not, then, a question, but a statement. It explains any delay in God's vindication of His elect on the basis of His patience, not His reluctance. The promise of a speedy vindication, given in verse 8, is thus qualified, in verse 7, by the reminder of God's long-suffering toward His people.

By mentioning God's patience, Jesus reminds God's elect, who are earnest in their prayer for vindication, that without an active faith the day of the Lord will be darkness and not light (Amos 5:18). Jesus concludes His parable with a challenging question for His followers. The imminence of the coming of the Son of man is here presupposed, but Jesus allows for an interval of time to pass. Will God's elect abandon their prayers and life of faith because they must endure a time of tribulation? The answer to that query depends entirely on us who "wait for the revealing of our Lord Jesus Christ" (1 Cor. 1:7).

CHAPTER 8

The Pharisee and the Tax Collector

Luke 18:9-14

9 He also told this parable to some who trusted in themselves that they were righteous and despised others: 10"Two men went up into the temple to pray, one a Pharisee and the other a tax collector. 11The Pharisee stood and prayed thus with himself, 'God, I thank thee that I am not like other men, extortioners, unjust, adulterers, or even like this tax collector. 12I fast twice a week, I give tithes of all that I get.' 13But the tax collector, standing far off, would not even lift up his eyes to heaven, but beat his breast, saying, 'God, be merciful to me a sinner!' 14I tell you, this man went down to his house justified rather than the other; for every one who exalts himself will be humbled, but he who humbles himself will be exalted."

Jesus liked to use the element of contrast in His parables. Consequently, in various of His stories we meet two figures, such as two sons (Luke 15:11), two debtors (chap. 7:41), or as in this case two worshipers (chap. 18:10). To appreciate the contrast in this parable, we must know to whom exactly the terms *Pharisee* and *publican* applied.

The English word *publican* comes from the Latin word *publicanus*, which means "a Roman tax official." The meaning "a keeper of a public house (hotel)" is a modern development. The *publicani* originally were individual entrepreneurs or syndicates who gained the right to gather the taxes from a certain district by tendering the highest bid. They were under the authority of the procurator (this means "imperial revenue official"), but there was little official interference. Since the publicans made their profits by levying an amount larger than the original bid, extortion was normal. The publicans were generally Roman capitalists from the equestrian class.

However, by the time of Jesus the original publicans no longer functioned in Palestine. Julius Caesar had put them out of business. Two new groups replaced them: tax collectors and toll collectors (for in addition to the direct taxes there were tolls, tariffs, and customs that had to be paid). Like the earlier publicans, the toll collectors were individual entrepreneurs who paid for the privilege of collecting the tolls. The word used in the Gospels means "buyer of tolls" and is translated in the King James Version as "publicans." The men we meet in the Gospels were the agents of the chief toll collectors. They were generally, therefore, Jews. They were the "small fry" of the system and came in for the immediate hatred of the populace. For a chosen nation, the tax collectors were the last obnoxious link in an intolerable chain. Most Jews believed that the tax collectors had abandoned their Judaism to serve the hated Romans.

The stigma that Jews attached to this hated trade is illustrated by the kinds of persons associated with the tax collectors in the Jewish and Christian sources. Jewish writings (for example, the Mishnah) couple tax collectors with thieves, robbers, money changers, Gentiles, and murderers. The Gospels extend the list, adding harlots (Matt. 21:31), robbers, swindlers, adulterers (Luke 18:11), and sinners (Matt. 9:11; Luke 19:7). Indeed, *tax collector* became a synonym for *sinner.* Modern research has found the tax collectors' practices no worse than those of regular businessmen of the time. Nevertheless, there can be little doubt that the invectives and hatred were, in the main, well deserved.

Tax collectors could not take out membership in the Pharisaic community, and if a Pharisee became one he was automatically expelled. Socially, tax collectors were officially ostracized and deprived of even the civil rights granted to bastards (considered a serious blemish). But Jesus, who was no politician or ecclesiastic, was quite indifferent to His public image. He shocked His contemporaries' sense of decency by calling a tax collector to be one of His disciples and by eating freely with other tax collectors.

The Pharisees were a religious group drawn from Jews of all social levels. They did not form a separate body like a denomination, but rather permeated the whole of Judaism. Strict rules bound the group together. It was an exclusive brotherhood, for they avoided contact with those whom they considered unclean or breakers of the law. This was especially evident in the matter of table fellowship. Generally they greeted (see Matt. 5:47) and ate only with one another. Their religious ideal was to fulfill the whole of Torah (the laws of the Pentateuch) and to apply the legal details to every aspect of daily life. In this they were innovators and not simply reactionary. Their zeal for the law included the traditional oral interpretations. Indeed, they revered what later became the rabbinic applications and discussions more than they respected the original Torah.

Josephus, the first-century Jewish historian, described the Pharisees in a way that coincides with the impression gained from the Gospels. He said that they were "a body of Jews who profess to be more religious than the rest and to explain the laws more precisely," "they pride themselves on the exact interpretation of the law of the fathers." They were, in a word, jealous protectors and observers of the unwritten laws.

A mass of careful rules regulated every facet of Jewish life: food and table fellowship, fasting and prayer, Sabbath and sacrifice, tithe and offering, birth and burial. The Pharisee did not consider the observance of these regulations a burden. To the contrary, the keeping of them he regarded as a joy and privilege. He was not generally a hypocrite. He was sincerely and truly pious. Unfortunately, the intensity of his religious piety could tend to make him bigoted.

Jesus had a deep respect for the Pharisees, but He relentlessly opposed their exclusiveness and pride. The parable of the publican and the Pharisee is one of Jesus' many attempts to jolt them into understanding. It is set in the Temple, most likely at the time of the morning or evening sarifice, when worshipers customarily assembled to pray (cf. Luke 1:8-10).

Luke 18:9-14 offers a searching description of the Pharisees. Jesus here addressed "some who trusted in themselves" (verse 9). The basis for their self-confidence was "that they were righteous," and the tragic result was that they "despised others" (verse 9). The Pharisee chose a prominent position (v. 11, T.E.V.) and offered thanks to God that by His grace he was not an extortioner, swindler, or adulterer. What prevented him from becoming like these despicables was the divine gift of the law that he delighted to keep.

His was no idle boast. The Pharisee proudly documented his no mean achievement as part of his prayer, which he probably spoke out loud. He had stood aside by himself so as to avoid any contaminating contact with the worshiping rabble, but he wanted them to hear his pious utterance. No doubt he thought his prayer would provide profitable instruction for their souls. He fasted twice each week. This greatly exceeded the five statutory fast days of the Jewish religion. It meant even going without water from sunrise to sunset, a considerable feat during the hot months. He paid tithe on his purchases, like corn and oil, in case the producer had neglected this duty. This was the mark of his piety; a Pharisee did more than was required.

Gratefully and truthfully he could thank God that he was "not like other men" (verse 11), for he outstripped his fellows in his devotion to the traditions of the fathers (see Gal. 1:14). He listed three typical examples of those whom he was thankfully not like—a rogue, a swindler, and an adulterer. He then turned to a specific fourth example—the nearby tax collector. The praying Pharisee prejudiced the tax collector's classification by listing him with these three disreputables. More than likely it was he whom the Pharisee wished to shame publicly with his audible exhortatory prayer, which was an admonition for the other worshipers, not an address to God.

What is wrong with the Pharisee's supplication? It was a sincere prayer of thanks, and that is praiseworthy. He went the second mile in fulfilling the law, and that is Biblical. The fault of the prayer is made apparent only by its contrast with the tax collector's petition. The Pharisee stood apart from the other worshipers to avoid contamination. The tax collector stood afar off because he felt defiled. The Jewish custom during prayer was to stand with eyes (see John 11:41; 17:1; Ps. 123:1) and hands (see Isa. 1:15) raised to heaven. The tax collector's sense of shame prevented him from lifting even his eyes to heaven (Luke 18:13). Rejected by his fellow Jews and condemned by himself, he prayed the only petition left to him—a prayer for God's mercy.

The tax collector smote himself over his heart (considered the seat of sin) as an act of repentance. Judaism stressed repentance as the indispensable route to atonement, but it was a difficult road for tariff agents. Repentance for them meant repayment of the embezzled sums, plus an extra one-fifth. They could never contact everyone they had cheated even if they had the cash. Consequently, the tax collector knew that he had no claim on God on the basis of merit. He implored God in penitential language drawn from Psalm 51:1. However, he used a different verb from that of the psalmist. The word he used is common in sacrificial contexts and means "to atone, expiate, propitiate." In the Temple setting the choice was appropriate. But his plea is best translated "Be favorable to me a sinner," as the sacrificial connotation is not to the fore.

Jesus' conclusion must surely have initially stunned and then angered His devout hearers (see Luke 18:1). A pious Jew and a greedy extortioner went up to pray, but the latter went down to his house justified rather than the former (verse 14). The Pharisee offered only thanksgiving. He felt no need for forgiveness. He sought to establish his own righteousness (see Rom. 10:3) and therefore missed the divine acquittal (see chap. 9:30, 31). The tax collector had nothing to boast before God (see chap. 4:2), so he trusted Him who justifies the ungodly (verse 5). In deep contrition he asked for divine favor, and he went down to his house in the clear with God. Both Jesus' and Paul's presentation of this unexpected reversal are daring.

Unlike the pharisee, the tax collector did not despise others. It was hardly a luxury one so abhorred as he could afford. However, it is easy, even while identifying with the tax collector, to thank God that we are not like the Pharisee. The modern tax collector sometimes prays, "Thank God I'm free from the law and not like other men—legalists, holy joes, sanctimonious saints, or even like this preacher here. I eat and drink my full and never give a dime to the church." When tax collectors despise others (even "Pharisees") with such superior tones, they too are praying the Pharisee's prayer. The true publican's prayer is "God, be merciful to me a sinner!" (Luke 18:13).

CHAPTER 9

The Unmerciful Servant

Matthew 18:23-35

23 "Therefore the kingdom of heaven may be compared to a king who wished to settle accounts with his servants. ²⁴When he began the reckoning, one was brought to him who owed him ten thousand talents; ²⁵and as he could not pay, his lord ordered him to be sold, with his wife and children and all that he had, and payment to be made. ²⁶So the servant fell on his knees, imploring him, 'Lord, have patience with me, and I will pay you everything.'²⁷And out of pity for him the lord of that servant released him and forgave him the debt. ²⁸But that same servant, as he went out, came upon one of his fellow servants who owed him a hundred denarii; and seizing him by the throat he said, 'Pay what you owe.'²⁹So his fellow servant fell down and besought him, 'Have patience with me, and I will pay you.'³⁰He refused and went and put him in prison till he should pay the debt. ³¹When his fellow servants saw what had taken place, they were greatly distressed, and they went and reported to their lord all that had taken place. ³²Then his lord summoned him

and said to him, 'You wicked servant! I forgave you all that debt because you besought me; [33]*and should not you have had mercy on your fellow servant, as I had mercy on you?'* [34]*And in anger his lord delivered him to the jailers, till he should pay all his debt.* [35]*So also my heavenly Father will do to every one of you, if you do not forgive your brother from your heart."*

The Father, Jesus informs us, causes the sun to rise on those who are evil as well as those who are good; He also sends the rain on the righteous and the unrighteous (Matt. 5:45). In other words, God is kind to the unthankful and to evildoers (Luke 6:35, K.J.V.). But how should the unthankful and the evildoers respond to God's kindness? What are the consequences if they respond in an unacceptable way?

The parable of the ungrateful servant (literally "a slave," possibly a slave with official or administrative status), which is found in Matthew 18:23-35, answers these questions in a graphic manner. The ultimate setting for this parable is the last judgment, but its practical objective is to challenge the Christian community in the present. The cultural background of the parable is not Jewish, but rather the despotic kingdoms of the surrounding Gentile world. The practices in these Hellenistic kingdoms were known to the Jews and, during the reign of Herod the Great, were even experienced by them.

A certain king decided to settle any outstanding accounts with his slave managers. Soon after he began the process of debt collection, a man was brought to him who owed him 10,000 talents. This is an enormous amount. Though such an astronomical sum is not unexampled in the ancient world, it is really a parabolic rather than a normal debt. For example, the total taxes collected in Judea, Idumea, and Samaria in 4 B.C. amounted to only 600 talents. Galilee's and Perea's tax in the same year was 200 talents. Herod's total annual income is estimated to have been between only 900 and 1,600 talents. In fact, 10,000 was the highest number used in reckoning in the Near East, and a talent was the largest monetary unit. Thus Jesus presents the picture of a slave-servant who was required to repay a loan (verse 27, Greek) of unimaginable size.

Not surprisingly the servant could not repay this extraordinary loan-debt. The king took an action that was common among non-Israelite rulers (cf. Isa. 50:1; Amos 2:6; 8:6; Neh. 5:1-13). He commanded the sale of the servant, his entire family, and all his possessions. Since slaves brought somewhere between 500 and 1,200 denarii on the market, and the servant owed 10,000 times 6,000 denarii (a talent equaled 6,000 denarii), it was impossible for the sale to equal the debt. To do so, the servant would need have been the progenitor of a very large household indeed.

The situation was desperate and grave. The slave begged his king for time in which to repay the loan (Matt. 18:26). This was an ironic Eastern hyperbolic touch. How could a poverty-stricken slave—no matter what his official status—hope to repay such an inconceivable debt, even if he were granted an infinite extension of time? Human sin incurs a debt that is likewise incalculable and beyond our resources to repay. The slave's desperate plea for time received a response from the king as unbelievable as the debt. The king felt compassion for the enormously in-debt servant and set him free, forgiving him his whole debt (verse 27).

All commercial societies have due legal processes for regaining bona fide debts. Without some legal protection, lenders would be at the mercy of every unscrupulous borrower. The first servant did nothing that was legally dishonorable (the harshness belonged to the times) when he foreclosed on a fellow servant who owed him some money (verses 28-30). Yet every interested reader feels the same grief that the man's fellow servants felt when they learned what this slave official had done (verse 31). They could easily see how the forgiven servant's action conflicted with his own immediately preceding experience.

It is the contrast between the king's merciful compassion and the servant's harsh demand for his legal right that condemns the latter's actions. The unmerciful servant had been freely released from a debt of 60 million denarii, and then he refused to deal kindly with a debt of 100 denarii (a ratio of 600,000 to 1). The inconsistency of the unmerciful servant's conduct is forcefully brought home by the fact that his debtor entreated him with language virtually the same as he himself had used when he beseeched the king for time to pay (see verses 26 and 29). His debtor also fell to his knees before him as he himself had done before the king.

Since a debt of 100 denarii was relatively easy to repay, the request for patience and time to repay was reasonable. The ungrateful servant had made the same request when his situation was, in contrast, virtually hopeless. Whereas he received more than he asked, he now gave less than was sought. Not only did he fail to remit the small debt as his own enormous debt had been forgiven, but he also failed even to grant an extension of time as requested. The ungrateful servant had his debtor thrown into prison.

The man's fellow servants reported his conduct to the king, who immediately sent for him. The king confronted the unmerciful servant with this embarrassing query: "You wicked servant! . . . Should not you have had mercy on your fellow servant, as I had mercy on you?" (verses 32, 33). The bumper sticker "Christians aren't perfect; they're only forgiven" does not say enough; one must add to the last clause, "and are forgiving."

Judaism believed that God assessed the world in the present with the dual measures of justice and mercy, but that at the last judgment He would use only the measure of justice. The Pharisees were confident that sheer justice would work in their favor. Jesus in this parable opposed this idea and taught that mercy too operates at the last judgment. But to whom is the measure of mercy granted? To the merciful. "Blessed are the merciful, for they shall obtain mercy [in the judgment]" (chap. 5:7); "If you forgive men their trespasses [now], your heavenly Father also will forgive you [in the judgment]" (chap. 6:14). "The measure you give [now] will be the measure you get [in the judgment]" (chap. 7:2).

The Christian's forgiveness does not, of course,

obtain the divine forgiveness. There is no barter. "We are not forgiven *because* we forgive, but *as* we forgive. The ground of all forgiveness is found in the unmerited love of God, but by our attitude toward others we show whether we have made that love our own."—*Christ's Object Lessons*, p. 251. The Christian is not simply to mouth the words of forgiveness, like an unrepentant little boy who is forced to utter "Sorry" by the will of his parent. The Christian is to forgive sincerely and tangibly from the heart (see chap. 18:35).

Such forgiveness is costly. There is nothing cheap about a grace that can move a Corrie ten Boom to forgive the Nazi guard who whipped her enfeebled sister Betsie (*The Hiding Place*, p. 191) or that can cause us to do good to those who despitefully treat us. The words of a popular song, "Though it makes Him sad to see the way we live, He'll always say 'I forgive,' " are an anemic statement of the Biblical doctrine of forgiveness. Forgiveness in the judgment is guaranteed only to those who are moved by the 10,000-talent divine mercy to forgive their 100-denarii debtors. A consistently opposite response will ultimately experience God's rejection (verses 34, 35).

In the pre-Advent judgment, Jesus defends His people against Satan's charges, "claiming for them forgiveness" (*The Great Controversy*, p. 484). Who are these for whom the Divine Advocate claims forgiveness? They are the grateful servants who responded to the remission of their massive debts by forgiving the comparatively smaller debts in their own sphere. In the words of Paul, which capture the message of this parable so well, they are those who are "kind to one another, tenderhearted, forgiving one another, as God in Christ forgave [them]" (Eph. 4:32). "As the Lord has forgiven you, so you also must forgive" (Col. 3:13).

CHAPTER 10

The Laborers in the Vineyard

Matthew 20:1-16

1 "For the kingdom of heaven is like a house-holder who went out early in the morning to hire laborers for his vineyard. ²After agreeing with the laborers for a denarius a day, he sent them into his vineyard. ³And going out about the third hour he saw others standing idle in the market place; ⁴and to them he said, 'You go into the vineyard too, and whatever is right I will give you.' So they went. ⁵Going out again about the sixth hour and the ninth hour, he did the same. ⁶And about the eleventh hour he went out and found others standing; and he said to them, 'Why do you stand here idle all day?' ⁷They said to him, 'Because no one has hired us.' He said to them, 'You go into the vineyard too.' ⁸And when evening came, the owner of the vineyard said to his steward, 'Call the laborers and pay them their wages, beginning with the last, up to the first.' ⁹And when those hired about the eleventh hour came, each of them received a denarius. ¹⁰Now when the first came, they thought they would receive more; but each of them also received a denarius. ¹¹And on receiving

*it they grumbled at the householder, ¹²saying,
'These last worked only one hour, and you have
made them equal to us who have borne the
burden of the day and the scorching heat.' ¹³But
he replied to one of them, 'Friend, I am doing you
no wrong; did you not agree with me for a
denarius? ¹⁴Take what belongs to you, and go; I
choose to give to this last as I give to you. ¹⁵Am I not
allowed to do what I choose with what belongs to
me? Or do you begrudge my generosity?' ¹⁶So the
last will be first, and the first last."*

A fair day's pay for a fair day's work is one of the
assumptions upon which our industrial society is
based. Workers have gone out on bitter strikes
because of disruptions in wage parity. Anything
that upsets the ratio between work done and pay
received offends our sense of industrial equity.
People in the ancient world also believed that there
should be a just proportion between labor and
reward. The proverbial saying "The laborer
deserves his wages" (1 Tim. 5:18; Luke 10:7)
admonishes employers to deal fairly with their
employees. Malpractice was condemned then as it
is now (James 5:1-6).

Jesus likened the kingdom of heaven to a
payday scene in which this common conviction
that wages should match the work done is flouted.
He reversed the old adage by telling a story that
appears to encourage the belief that it is "better late
than early." The fact that Jesus contradicted the
usual idea of a just settlement warns us that He was
not addressing the issue of industrial ethics. Bruce
Barton *(The Man Nobody Knows)* is way off when

he argues that Jesus laid down the rules for succeeding in business.

It is difficult not to feel some sympathy with the workers who complained, "You have made them equal to us who have borne the burden of the day and the scorching heat" (Matt. 20:12). That the parable offends our natural sense of fair play forewarns us that Jesus' idea of grace is radical. Jesus did not believe that God's ways could be accurately described in the neat and balanced calculations of an accountant.

The parable commences with a comparison, "The kingdom of heaven is like a householder who . . ." (verse 1). This is a standard opening. For example, "The kingdom of heaven may be compared to a man who sowed . . ." (chap. 13:24), "The kingdom of heaven may be compared to a king who . . ." (chap. 18:23; also chaps. 13:31, 33, 44, 45, 47; 22:2; 25:1). The kingdom of heaven is likened not simply to a sower, a king, ten maidens, or a householder, but to what each of these does. In Matthew 20:1-16 Jesus likened the kingdom of heaven (God's inbreaking rule) to an estate owner who wanted to hire laborers to harvest his crop of grapes. This winegrower went out at dawn to engage day laborers for the task. He and the workers agreed to a rate of one denarius per day, the usual daily wage.

Approximately at 9:00 A.M., noon, and 3:00 P.M. the owner again visited the marketplace and offered employment to any whom he found standing idly by. Since they were hired late, they were not eligible for a full day's pay. The employer, therefore, promised to give them a fair rate (verse 4). Those engaged at 9:00 A.M., noon, and 3:00 P.M. are not referred to again in the parable. Jesus' mention of them coveys an atmosphere of haste, though one suggestion is that the sentence "So they went" (verse 4) means they refused employment and ambled off. Whatever the explanation, it produces the literary effect of an ascending climax. Finally, at the eleventh hour (about 5:00 P.M.), only one hour before quitting time, the householder engaged another group of workers.

In this latter instance there was no negotiation, and so presumably payment depended as previously on the householder's discretion (verse 4). They probably expected an hour's pay (one twelfth of a day's wage), for this would fulfill the farmer's promise to pay "whatever is right" (verse 4). At evening, in accordance with Israelite law (Lev. 19:13; Deut. 24:15), the estate owner instructed his manager to pay all the hired men, beginning with the last and then finally ending with those engaged at dawn. The men who had worked for only one hour were pleasantly surprised to receive a full day's pay, a denarius. When the others who had worked for twelve hours saw this, they quickly recalculated their own salary at the new rate. They concluded that under the new award they would receive the staggering sum of twelve denarii. As Scripture nicely states it: "They thought they would receive more" (Matt. 20:10).

"But each of them also received a denarius" (verse 10). Those whom the winegrower hired last had worked only a fraction of the time, yet they had received an equal wage with those who had labored all day. The grumbling of the longtime workers, therefore, seems reasonable. Their complaint was twofold. First, they were disgruntled that the householder had made no pecuniary distinction between twelve hours of work and one hour of work. And second, they felt that he had entirely ignored the difference between only working in the cool of the evening and enduring the scorching heat of the whole day (verse 12). They apparently had a good case.

The landowner picked out the belligerents' spokesman (see verse 13) and asked him three irrefutable questions.

1. "Did you not agree with me for a denarius?" (verse 13). There was no denying this. The grumblers could not accuse the householder of breach of contract. The good employer correctly reminded their leader, "Friend, I am doing you no wrong" (verse 13).

2. "Am I not allowed to do what I choose with what belongs to me?" (verse 15). A claim like this usually defends some selfish desire to do what one wants with one's own. The householder, however, used this question to support his right to be generous.

3. "Do you begrudge my generosity?" (verse 15). The disgruntled, of course, did not begrudge the employer's generosity. Their complaint was that others less deserving than themselves had been recipients of it. As far as they were concerned, the issue was the justice of the episode, not his generosity.

Is God, then, unfair? In C. S. Lewis' *Till We Have Faces,* Queen Orual exclaimed, "Are the gods not just?" To our relief her tutor replied, "Oh, no, child. What would become of us if they were?" The point of Jesus' parable is that God is good, that He gives His love generously to the undeserving. Those who had worked for only one hour could make no valid demand for a day's wage. They could only leave themselves to the employer's generosity. God's goodness is not something that is portioned out with the exactitude of an industrial arbiter. As T. W. Manson reminds us: "There is such a thing as the twelfth part of a denar. It was called a pondion. But there is no such thing as a twelfth part of the love of God."—*The Sayings of Jesus*, p. 220.

Jesus' view of grace contrasted starkly with the outlook of the Pharisees. "The reward of the righteous they hoped to gain by their own works."—*Christ's Object Lessons*, p. 390. On the basis of justice alone they expected to gain an entrance into the kingdom of God. Jesus' own conduct demonstrated that God's attitude to the undeserving is generous. The Pharisees, like the discontented laborers in the parable, grumbled at this. A similar rabbinic parable from the fourth century A.D. throws the difference between Jesus and the Pharisees into sharp relief.

A certain Rabbi Bun bar Hijja died very young, and one of his colleagues gave the funeral address in the form of the following parable. A certain king hired a group of laborers. Two hours later he noticed that one of them had vastly outstripped the others in industry. He invited this hard worker to join him as he strolled. When evening came the king paid them all a day's wage, including the one who had labored industriously for two hours. Those who had labored all day murmured at this.

But the king replied, "He has done more work in two hours than you have done during the whole day." The funeral orator, Rabbi Zeira, then drew his conclusion: "Though Rabbi Bun bar Hijja had died at only 28 years, his short life was so industrious in the study of the law that he merited an equal reward with any scholar who died at a ripe old age."

The rabbinic parable is eager to demonstrate that, despite appearances, the laborer who had worked only briefly fully deserved his wages. Jesus' story, in contrast, frankly stresses the last-hired employees' lack of deserts. They received full pay solely because of the householder's generosity. The ideas of the two parables are poles apart. This is further illustrated by another rabbinic parable of the fourth century A.D. with a similar plot. In this parable Israel is identified with those who worked long, and the Gentiles with those who labored briefly. The story concludes, "The people of the world have accomplished very little for me, and I will give them but a small reward. You [Israel], however, will receive a large recompense."

Jesus stands this attitude on its head. He declares, "The last will be first, and the first last" (Matt. 20:16). Because entrance into the kingdom is a matter of divine grace, the lowly and recent disciples of Christ precede those who thought they had some privileged status (see chap. 19:28, 30).

Likewise, the Gentiles are not disadvantaged with respect to the Jews. God's generous grace makes the length of national service an irrelevance. Boasting is excluded, for the reward is unmerited. The householder's dealing with the workers represents God's dealing with the world. Thankfully "it is contrary to the customs that prevail among men" (*Christ's Object Lessons,* p. 397), and "depends not upon man's will or exertion, but upon God's mercy" (Rom. 9:16).

The parable of the laborers in the vineyard is thus a defense of Jesus' gospel. God is like the generous employer, for He sends His rain on the just and unjust alike (Matt. 5:45). Jesus disputes the Pharisees' exacting commercial analogy of salvation, in which God is thought to treat the world with a ledger-like exactitude. On the contrary, God's methods of payment have little analogy with sound economic practice. Jesus' teaching challenges the Pharisees and us not only to experience God's kindness to the undeserving but also to practice it.

CHAPTER 11

The Ten Maidens Awaiting a Wedding

Matthew 25:1-13

1 *"Then the kingdom of heaven shall be compared to ten maidens who took their lamps and went to meet the bridegroom. ²Five of them were foolish, and five were wise. ³For when the foolish took their lamps, they took no oil with them; ⁴but the wise took flasks of oil with their lamps. ⁵As the bridegroom was delayed, they all slumbered and slept. ⁶But at midnight there was a cry, 'Behold, the bridegroom! Come out to meet him.' ⁷Then all those maidens rose and trimmed their lamps. ⁸And the foolish said to the wise, 'Give us some of your oil, for our lamps are going out.' ⁹But the wise replied, 'Perhaps there will not be enough for us and for you; go rather to the dealers and buy for yourselves.' ¹⁰And while they went to buy, the bridegroom came, and those who were ready went in with him to the marriage feast; and the door was shut. ¹¹Afterward the other maidens came also, saying, 'Lord, lord, open to us.' ¹²But he replied, 'Truly, I say to you, I do not know you.' ¹³Watch therefore, for you know neither the day nor the hour."*

In our modern society we generally associate weddings with a formal service in a church. The organist plays. The assembled guests may sing hymns. The minister preaches a sermon. And prayers are said. In Biblical times, weddings were domestic affairs. They were sacred acts then as now, but they took place in the home, not the synagogue.

Although customs varied, a regular feature was a flaming torchlight procession from the bride's home to the bridegroom's (or his parents') house. The bridegroom with a group of his friends arrived at the bride's home to receive his suitably veiled and bedecked bride, who would accompany him to his home. The bride's friends joined the groom's group, with flaming lamps held aloft and with much singing, the happy bridal pair proceeded to the nuptial feast.

The lamps that the ten maidens used in Jesus' story were probably not the small terra-cotta lamps that were suitable only indoors. The kind more likely to have been used in an outdoor procession would consist of a copper bowl that was filled with olive oil and rags and fastened to a pole. The amount of fuel needed to keep the small terra-cotta lamps burning was meager, but the torches required a good supply of oil.

Jesus described five of the maidens as foolish and five as wise. What was it that warranted this distinction?

Matthew frequently uses the technique of contrast: two builders (chap. 7:24-27), two kinds of seed (chap. 13:24-30), two types of fish (verses 47-49), two sons (chap. 21:28-32), two men (chap.

24:40), two women (verse 41), two servants (verses 45-51), two kinds of flocks (chap. 25:31-46). The essence of the contrast in several of these examples turns on doing or not doing. One builder builds on sand; the other, on a rock. The latter refers to those who both hear and do Jesus' words (chap. 7:24), and the other refers to those who hear but do not do (verse 26). The wheat and the tares and the good and bad fish refer to the evil and the righteous (chap. 13:49). The two sons also contrast merely saying and not doing with the actual doing of the father's will (see chap. 21:31). The faithful servant does his master's command, while the wicked servant, of course, does not (chap. 24:45, 46, 48, 49). The sheep ("the righteous" [chap. 25:37]) do deeds of mercy to the least of the Lord's brethren (verses 35, 36, 40); the goats do not (verses 42, 43, 45).

Each wise maiden took along a flask of oil in addition to her lamp. The foolish maidens did not. Also we notice two aspects related to the bridegroom's arrival: It was delayed, and then it came suddenly at an unexpected hour. The five wise virgins were prepared for just such a delay. What distinguished the wise from the foolish builder was that the wise man was ready for the sudden flood and the foolish man was not (chap. 7:24-27). Likewise the wise and faithful servant continued to do his master's will, even though his master's return was delayed, but the wicked servant made the delay an occasion for evildoing. The sudden and unexpected return of the master found the wicked servant unprepared (chap. 24:48-50).

Because the wise maidens had extra oil, the

delay or the sudden cry that the bridegroom was coming (chap. 25:6) did not leave them embarrassed. The builder who built on the rock did Jesus' word and is called wise because he was thus prepared for the flood. The servant who did his master's will, even when the master was delayed, is called wise because his obedience made him ready for the master's sudden return. Similarly the five maidens are called wise because they were ready for the bridegroom's arrival whether it was swift or delayed.

The five wise maidens were ready beause they had sufficient oil to sustain a delay in the awaited event. The wise builder and the wise servant are called wise because their faithful doing of the deeds of the kingdom made them ready for a sudden event (in the former case of flood, and in the latter a master's return). The wise virgins represent those who persevere in well-doing while awaiting the Bridegroom. They are prepared by "the golden oil of goodness, patience, long-suffering, gentleness, [and] love" (*Testimonies to Ministers,* p. 511) for the return of Christ.

The coming of the Son of man is a basic theme in what is usually termed the fifth discourse, that is, Matthew 23-25. One feature of this Advent is the fact that it can occur at any time (see, for example, chap. 24:36, 37, 42-44, 50, 51). Another element is delay (see verses 34, 48; chap. 25:19). Both these aspects are present in the parable of the ten virgins. The slumbering of all ten maidens should not, then, be understood as allegorically portraying the church's spiritual lethargy; rather, it graphically conveys the fact that the Bridegroom's arrival is delayed (chap. 25:5). The cry comes at midnight (verse 6), when all the maidens are naturally asleep, which indicates the suddenness and unexpectedness of the Bridegroom's arrival: "In the evening, or at midnight, or at cockcrow, or in the morning—lest he come suddenly and find you asleep" (Mark 13:35, 36).

Clearly for Matthew, if anyone is ultimately to be vindicated in the last judgment, then love must not wax cold (chap. 24:12, 13), good works must be seen (chap. 5:16), saying must be followed by doing (chaps. 7:24, 25; 21:28-31; 23:3), and good fruit must be borne (chaps. 3:8; 21:43). To have sufficient oil is to have "by faith the golden oil of love [that] flows freely, to shine out again in good works, in real, heartfelt service for God" (*Christ's Object Lessons*, p. 419). This is not legalism, but a compassionate doing of Jesus' teaching—a doing that is begotten and moved by the prior salvation through Jesus.

The word *foolish* in Matthew indicates one who is outside or ignorant of the kingdom (see chaps. 5:22; 7:26; 23:17). The fool may profess discipleship, but it is merely a matter of words. The foolish virgins follow Christ in word only, and therefore they receive the same denunciation that the fruitless but vocal false prophets received (chap. 7:15-23): "I do not know you" (chap. 25:12; cf. chap. 7:23). To be without sufficient oil is to be like a tree without good fruit (chap. 7:19), or a wedding guest without the festive attire (chap. 22:11-13), or a servant without interest on his master's capital (chap. 25:24-30), that is, to be without the deeds of the gospel. And every servant who lacks these deeds is condemned in the judgment (chaps. 7:19; 22:13; 25:11, 12, 30).

The sudden arrival of the bridegroom quickly made the foolish maidens aware of their unpreparedness. Their mere membership in the group did not amount to anything without oil, that is, without an active discipleship. Their efforts to borrow and to purchase oil proved fruitless. They were on their own, and they were not ready. Those who were ready entered into the marriage feast, while the foolish maidens scurried frantically around, only to find upon reaching the banquet hall that "the door was shut" (verse 10). As C. S. Lewis poignantly observed, "When the author walks onto the stage the play is over."—*Mere Christianity*, p. 63. To attempt to produce the fruits of discipleship when the Lord comes is too late. "The night is far gone, the day is at hand. Let us then cast off the works of darkness and put on the armor of light" (Rom. 13:12). "Let us be sober, and put on the breastplate of faith and love" (1 Thess. 5:8).

The ten virgins stand for the Christian community—a community that has received the goodness of God in the salvation of Jesus and that now awaits His return. Only those members of the fellowship who observe and do the teaching of Jesus, with its emphasis on mercy and forgiveness, will be declared true disciples in the last judgment. To receive the gospel of Jesus is to live the gospel, and to live the gospel means to bear the fruits of the gospel—love, joy, mercy, grace, forgiveness, peace. For those who know the gospel will be judged by the gospel.

CHAPTER 12

The Sheep and the Goats

Matthew 25:31-46

31 "When the Son of man comes in his glory, and all the angels with him, then he will sit on his glorious throne. ³²Before him will be gathered all the nations, and he will separate them one from another as a shepherd separates the sheep from the goats, ³³and he will place the sheep at his right hand, but the goats at the left. ³⁴Then the King will say to those at his right hand, 'Come, O blessed of my Father, inherit the kingdom prepared for you from the foundation of the world; ³⁵for I was hungry and you gave me food, I was thirsty and you gave me drink, I was a stranger and you welcomed me, ³⁶I was naked and you clothed me, I was sick and you visited me, I was in prison and you came to me.' ³⁷Then the righteous will answer him, 'Lord, when did we see thee hungry and feed thee, or thirsty and give thee drink? ³⁸And when did we see thee a stranger and welcome thee, or naked and clothe thee? ³⁹And when did we see thee sick or in prison and visit thee?' ⁴⁰And the King will answer them, 'Truly, I say to you, as you did it to one of the least of these my brethren, you

did it to me.' ⁴¹Then he will say to those at his left hand, 'Depart from me, you cursed, into the eternal fire prepared for the devil and his angels; ⁴²for I was hungry and you gave me no food, I was thirsty and you gave me no drink, ⁴³I was a stranger and you did not welcome me, naked and you did not clothe me, sick and in prison and you did not visit me.' ⁴⁴Then they also will answer, 'Lord, when did we see thee hungry or thirsty or a stranger or naked or sick or in prison, and did not minister to thee?' ⁴⁵Then he will answer them, 'Truly, I say to you, as you did it not to one of the least of these, you did it not to me.' ⁴⁶And they will go away into eternal punishment, but the righteous into eternal life."

Epicurus was right: "What men fear is not that death is annihilation, but that it is not." Judgment, if we are honest, is an unnerving prospect. There are scriptures enough to warrant some discomfort. For example, ponder the following: "It is a fearful thing to fall into the hands of the living God" (Heb. 10:31). "If we sin deliberately after receiving the knowledge of the truth, there no longer remains a sacrifice for sins, but a fearful prospect of judgment" (verses 26, 27). "God is a consuming fire" (chap. 12:29). "There will be tribulation and distress for every human being who does evil" (Rom. 2:9). "On the day of judgment men will render account for every careless word they utter" (Matt. 12:36). There is no shortage of such texts, and they are too serious to permit complacency.

Some at this point may wish to urge us, as Mrs.

Adams did Dr. Samuel Johnson, not "to forget the merits of our Redeemer." But we should also recall Johnson's reply: "Madam, I do not forget the merits of my Redeemer; but my Redeemer has said that He will set some on His right hand and some on His left."—Boswell's *Life of Samuel Johnson*, vol. II, p. 526. There *is* a left side, and Jesus described the destiny of those on it in fearful terms: "Depart . . . into the eternal fire prepared for the devil and his angels" (chap. 25:41). There is little comfort in the thought that the offer of a mere cup of water gets one onto the right side, for the neglect of the same simple act puts one onto the left. Perhaps you noticed that Jesus' parable follows a careful, if repetitive, balance.

The reading of the parable immediately raises two questions:

1. What is meant by "all the nations" (verse 32)?

2. To whom does the phrase "one of the least of these my brethren" (verse 40; cf. verse 45) refer?

The first question seems initially to allow only one reply, namely, all the people who have ever lived. However, one scholar recently noted that the cursed, as well as the blessed, address the Son of man as Lord (verse 44). The scholar therefore argued that "all the nations" must refer to those Gentiles who have responded, no matter how partially, to the Christian world mission. This view is not compelling because " ' "Lord" ' " is the only appropriate address in the parable, where the Son of man is pictured as a king (verses 34, 40). Matthew's total usage of the phrase "all the nations" makes the meaning here clear.

In Matthew's Greek the plural phrase "the

nations" (chaps. 4:15; 6:32; 10:5, 18; 12:18, 21; 20:19, 25) always refers to the Gentiles in distinction to Israel. The expanded form "all the nations" occurs only in missionary settings (see chaps. 24:9, 14; 28:19; cf. chap. 10:18). It is safe to conclude that "all the nations" refers especially to the Gentiles, for they are the object of the Christian missionary witness. But because the Christian mission began with the religious rejects ("lost") of Israel (chap. 10:5-15), Israel should not be entirely excluded from this judgment scene.

If "all the nations," or the Gentiles, are the people of the world who are confronted by the Christian testimony, who are "the least of these my brethren"? The traditional view is that Jesus here refers to the poor, the oppressed, the needy, of the world. Without our denying that such classes are the worthy objects of Christian love, it is doubtful whether this is the true meaning of Matthew 25:40 and 45. Again the safest procedure is to examine parallel passages in Matthew. Consider the following list: "least in the kingdom of heaven" (chap. 11:11); "one of these little ones [least] who believe in me" (chap. 18:6); "do not despise one of these little ones" (verse 10); "that one of these little ones should perish" (verse 14).

Each of these examples refers to the most insignificant, weakest, or most vulnerable of Jesus' disciples. This basically is also the meaning in Matthew 25:40, 45. There is a very close bond between Jesus and His powerless followers. Thus, any person of the nations who supports Christians in their mission—even with a cup of water—and do not take advantage of their weakness by abusing them, do it unto Jesus. Such individuals will receive their reward. Their kindness to helpless Christian missionaries is nothing other than the reception of Christ and the gospel.

The acceptance of a lowly Christian is the reception of Christ (chap. 18:5). This is especially true of the missionary disciple. The apostolic mendicant preachers were entirely dependent on the hospitality of the townspeople they visited (see chap. 10:9-14). As the gospel was their only power, they often endured abuse, including imprisonment and even death (see verses 16-23; chap. 24:9, 10). Anyone who aided such bearers of the gospel, when it was popular and easy to harass them, aided Christ: "He who receives you receives me" (chap. 10:40). Very significant for the understanding of this parable is the following statement of Jesus: "Whoever gives to one of these little ones [least] even a cup of cold water because he is a disciple, truly, I say to you, he shall not lose his reward" (verse 42).

Consequently, those who were hungry, thirsty, a stranger, naked, sick, or imprisoned were not the general needy of the world, but the persecuted itinerant Christian missionaries to the Gentiles. Such were jailed because of their testimony concerning Christ, not because of any criminal activity. Their state of poverty and reliance on local generosity belonged to their apostolic office. The rigors of their task often left them naked, penniless, and sick. The outstanding example in the New Testament of these "least" brethren is the apostle Paul. Practically the same deprivations enumerated in Matthew 25:35, 36 are also found in his descriptions of his ministry: "To the present hour we hunger and thirst, we are ill-clad and buffeted and homeless" (1 Cor. 4:11; see also 2 Cor. 6:4-10; 11:23-29).

Some scholars suggest that the righteous confess surprise at Jesus' praise (Matt. 25:37-39) because, as true Christians, they did their good works without any thought of personal merit. The fact is that the righteous are not Christians but Gentiles. They are righteous Gentiles because they welcomed Christ in the person of His lowly ministers. Their surprise, therefore, is due to the fact that they did not know that their assistance of a destitute stranger would be counted as done to the latter's Lord.

The cursed (verse 41), like the righteous, also manifest bewilderment at the king's recital. But in this case it is because of their neglect of him. One scholar believes that this is because they are Christians and expect to receive a welcome entrance into their Lord's kingdom. But clearly they are also Gentiles, and their surprise results from their not knowing that their rejection of a mendicant missionary meant rejecting Christ. Unlike the Christians who are shocked at their final rejection (see chap. 7:21-23), these do not argue their case with a catalog of their mighty deeds. What they utter is the query "When?" (chap. 25:44), not the argument "Did we not?" (chap. 7:22). There is thus a clear distinction between the rejected disciples in Matthew 7:21-23 and the cursed men and women in this parable.

People in the world where the gospel goes are judged by how they receive the "little ones" (nobodies!) who carry it. For they "are the aroma of

Christ to God . . ., to one a fragrance from death to death, to the other a fragrance from life to life" (2 Cor. 2:15, 16). How those among the nations treat the least disciple is the real evidence of their acceptance or rejection of the gospel.

What of those who live in regions where no missionary has penetrated? Or what happens to those who have never had an opportunity of tangibly helping one of these least of His brethren? Matthew asserts only the serious consequences attached to slighting those connected with the apostolic world mission. He says nothing of people outside its pale. Without reducing the urgency of the evangelistic commission, their destiny must be left to the fairness of God. (See Luke 12:47, 48.)

If you feel that this parable of the sheep and the goats gives the missionary an excessively exalted role, several facts should be borne in mind. First, the apostolic witness was carried by men and women who were generally poorer and more defenseless than their modern counterparts. To show compassion to such social vagabonds revealed a real heeding of the gospel. Second, the traveling preachers were but as clay pots ("least"). Response to them was crucial only because they were emissaries of Christ. Third, elsewhere Matthew shifts his focus from the judgment of the nations to the judgment of Jesus' disciples (Matt. 7:21-23; 25:14-30). They have no grounds for feeling cocksure. Fourth, the role of the traveling preachers was not an exalted one. Instead, they experienced suffering and pain for Christ's sake. Hence His identity with them.

One must not imagine that the cup of water

given to these despised ambassadors of the gospel was merely a casual and simple service such as any tourist would receive. The righteous tended their help at some danger and cost to themselves. No doubt their act evoked some hostility from their peers. The parable is not just teaching decent behavior, worthy as that is. It reminds the disciples that Christ is in the world through them. Their treatment of the Christian missionary, Jesus transfers to Himself. Men and women acknowledge Him or despise Him depending on how they relate to His most insignificant servants (see chaps. 10:32, 33; 12:30).

Epilogue

The preceding studies reveal how surprising some of Jesus' images of God and the kingdom are. A waster son is banqueted. A cheat is praised and justified. Righteous men are rebuked. Slackers are rewarded. Enemies are presented as models. An unjust judge, an indulgent father, and an unresponsive friend are used to depict God. This colorful diction is not merely for rhetorical show. Jesus' idea of God and His grace may seem to be as radical as His stories.

The parables powerfully defend Jesus' conviction that God graciously accepts tax collectors, prostitutes, Samaritans, and sinners before they accept Him. In addition, the parables challenge the righteous to share in and practice the divine compassion. This does not mean that Jesus advocates God's love as a cover under which one could sin without feeling guilty. God's love, according to Jesus, is as demanding as it is free. But Jesus is no guardian of the religious idiosyncrasies that are so precious to the pious. Discipleship is not a matter of an ascetic life or secret wisdom. Rather, discipleship involves radically living out the compassion, forgiveness, and mercy of God that we receive in the gospel.

The parables are not merely charming tales. Beyond their immediate simplicity they convey profound theological messages. True, theirs is not the intricate construction of philosophical theology. Nevertheless, they are theological. Indeed, constantly our study has discovered a strong unity between Jesus' teaching and Paul's. However, Jesus did not develop some abstract doctrinal system. His parables formed part of His dialogic cut and thrust with His contemporaries. He used them to trouble religious smugness and call the just as well as sinners to a decision. Jesus did not make prolonged and emotional evangelistic appeals. The genius of His parables is that they leave the hearers with troublesome challenges to ponder. The nature of the parables sets truth in a story, and this gives them their unique power to nag persistently the conscience.

It is very dangerous to conflict with and to challenge religious prejudice. The spiritual leaders of Jesus' day avoided the troublesome questions by crucifying the Questioner. And that became His greatest parable.